FHM

Get **more** out of libraries

Please return or renew this item by the last date shown.

You can renew online at www.hants.gov.uk/library

Or by phoning 0300 555 1387

Hampshire
County Council

ESSENTIAL
MANAGERS
SELLING

DK

Written by Eric Baron

Senior Art Editor Gillian Andrews
Project Editor Hugo Wilkinson
Designer XAB Design
Editor Louise Tucker
US Editors Margaret Parrish, Jill Hamilton
Managing Editor Gareth Jones
Senior Managing Art Editor Lee Griffiths
Production Editor Nikoleta Parasaki
Production Controller Mandy Inness
Jacket Designer Mark Cavanagh
Design Development Manager Sophia M.T.T.

Delhi Team:
Senior Editorial Manager Rohan Sinha
Deputy Managing Art Editor Sudakshina Basu

First published in 2009 by
Dorling Kindersley Limited
80 Strand
London WC2R 0RL
A Penguin Random House Company

15 16 17 18 10 9 8 7 6 5 4 3 2 1

001-279395-May/2015

A CIP catalogue record for this book
is available from the British Library.

ISBN 978-0-2411-8636-7

Colour reproduction by
Colourscan, Singapore
Printed in China

www.dk.com

Contents

Introduction   6

Chapter 1
**Building meaningful
relationships**   **8**

Adding value through selling   10
Addressing needs   14
Appealing to buyers   16
Differentiating yourself   22

Chapter 2
**Understanding the
needs of customers**   **24**

Implementing the model   26
Recognizing needs   28
Planning your approach   34
Making your first move   36
Presenting your credentials   38
Opening a sales meeting   40
Questioning for needs   42
Listening to your client   48
Approaching a problem   50
Reviewing needs   52
Running a joint meeting   54

Chapter 3
Recommending solutions   **56**

Using features and benefits   58
Targeting the pitch   60
Offering your ideas   62
Asking for feedback   64

Chapter 4
Concluding the sale   **66**

Understanding objections   68
Collecting the data   72
Reframing objections   78
Discussing price   80
Responding to objections   84
Closing the sale   86
Moving beyond the close   92

Index   94
Acknowledgments   96

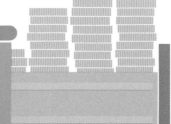

Introduction

Selling is one of the world's oldest professions, and one that constantly moves with, and adapts to, broader changes in business practice, human interactions, and psychology. Selling is also – as every salesperson will tell you – at the cutting edge of every business. Without the eyes, ears, and intuition of a good salesperson, the business itself founders.

Every good salesperson knows their products inside-out – whether these are paper clips, aircraft engines, or consultancy services – and can present them capably to their customers. However, a great salesperson does much more. He or she understands their customers' needs, and brings a problem-solving mentality and real creativity to their interactions.

Selling is all about combining a set of attitudes, behaviours, and skills in a way that forges long-term relationships with customers – relationships that add value to the customer's business and that yield not just one agreed deal, but many.

Despite some bad press over the years, selling is an honourable profession. The aim of this book is to open your mind to help you approach selling in a very different way and to introduce the skills that you must demonstrate every day. Let the journey begin!

Building
meaningful
relationships

People buy from people whom they like, respect, and trust, so selling is really about building and managing relationships. The first step is to find out what your customers expect and demand, and what you need to do to respond accordingly.

10 | ADDING VALUE THROUGH SELLING

14 | ADDRESSING NEEDS

16 | APPEALING TO BUYERS

22 | DIFFERENTIATING YOURSELF

01

Adding value through selling

Offering good products at competitive prices just isn't enough to win sales in today's competitive market. You can be sure that your best ideas will be emulated by others sooner or later. Today's customers expect you to add value to their business – to address their needs and deliver solutions.

Selling today

Being a successful salesperson today involves you in collaboration, facilitation, and a sense of partnership with your customer. Long gone are the days of one-way persuasion – the canned pitch is considered the lowest level of selling. Ideas about selling have evolved rapidly as globalization and fast communication through social media have produced more savvy and demanding buyers. Selling reflects much wider changes in business and goes far beyond pushing a product. Today, selling embraces a wide range of skills – a good understanding of how organizations work, management structures, psychology, and a level of self-awareness.

Tip

THINK CREATIVE
Don't limit yourself to **thinking** only about your products and services – your customers need your **creativity** to help **solve their problems**.

Globalization and **fast** communication have produced more demanding **buyers**

Understanding your role

In the past, salespeople could get by easily; they eloquently told the customer everything they knew about their product, explaining why their company was the best in its field. This approach may still win you business today in some areas, but most customers now demand much more from their salespeople. They expect salespeople to add value to their business – to fully understand their needs and to offer solutions to problems they didn't even realize they had.

66%

of **sales managers** believe that **selling in terms of value** rather than price is **essential for success**

Gaining skills

To succeed, you need to interpret what the client tells you, and often educate your customer about what's out there. Then you need to mesh together the abilities of your organization with that of the client for the benefit of both. You need a measure of curiosity and good listening skills to uncover what the client really needs. And you must be a brilliant innovator, with the ability to think creatively, and manage creative processes that find answers.

Being a good salesperson

There's no formula for a great salesperson – they come from all walks of life and levels of society. Salespeople tend to be naturally gifted problem-solvers, and share other innate characteristics that make them more likely to succeed.

Salespeople tend to be naturally **gifted problem-solvers**

A thick skin – knowing how to deal with failure, and understanding that even the best lose more often than they win a sale. With experience, most salespeople do learn how to deal with the inevitable negative responses to their ideas, as well as how to control their own innate emotional responses to knockbacks.

Generosity – giving credit to others where it is deserved without reservation or hesitation, and sharing the credit without any fear of diminishing their own individual contribution to the sale.

Willingness to take risks – putting their own necks on the line and entering unchartered ground to come up with unique ideas.

85% of the **top salespeople** questioned in one survey were found to be **conscientious**

A methodical approach – understand that planning and follow-up are the keys to success.

Tenacity – knowing that they need effort and determination to tackle daunting problems.

Resourcefulness – constantly innovating and challenging the existing approaches. Salespeople work well in groups and make the most of the talent around them.

Addressing needs

Selling isn't a moment of inspiration; it is not about force of argument or the strength of your personality. It is a process. The process is fairly easy to understand, but – as you'll see – hard to do. The techniques in this book are centred around a process called needs-based selling, so let's examine its principles and set the scene.

Examining the process

The process of selling needs careful planning and management. Beginning a relationship with a new client is the first phase of the process: you can't just walk into a customer's office and start a sales meeting. The first meeting needs careful staging, and both you and your customer need to be prepared.

Presenting confidently

Next, you start the most important part of the sales process – determining the customer's needs. During this phase, you ask the key questions, listen to what the customer has to say, identify both the obvious and less obvious needs, enter into a meaningful dialogue, and review the facts you have learned. Needs determination drives everything in

> **Tip**
>
> ### REFRAME THE SALES VISIT
> Think of every sales call as a **problem-solving** opportunity. You are selling more than products and services; you're selling ideas, **perspectives, and insights**.

selling, and it is only once you have listened to your customer that you move on to the phase of the process that most salespeople enjoy the most: presenting their products and services. This is when you are able to explain how you and your company can address your customer's needs. You know your products and services inside-out, and your customers want to hear how you can help them.

Winning commitment

Once you have determined the needs and made recommendations, it is time to think about gaining commitment. But something almost always gets in the way – and you face resistance to commit. The customer needs to be allowed to object – even when they seem ready to buy – and you must resolve all the client's objections if you are to close the sale.

52%

of customers in one survey **valued** companies who made it easy to **ask questions**

Needs-based selling

Simply put, needs-based selling means determining a customer's needs before you start to propose solutions. Get to understand the customer by letting them speak. When it's time to present, you will do a better job than those who only display their products and services and you'll be far better positioned to sustain a long-term relationship with your customer.

Solving problems

Success in selling is linked to effective problem solving. If you're good at one technique, the chances are that you will excel at the other. The process of problem solving is also remarkably similar in its structure to that of selling. The following chart shows these similarities at each stage of the process.

Comparing problem solving with selling

PROBLEM SOLVING	STEP	NEEDS-BASED SELLING
Set the stage. Provide structure for the problem-solving session.	01	**Open the meeting**. Build rapport, confirm the agenda, and prepare the customer.
Define the problem. Review background information and solutions already tried.	02	**Determine needs**. Engage with the client and tease out both their obvious and their hidden needs.
Generate ideas. Provide the climate where everyone can contribute creative perspectives without judgement.	03	**Present products** and services, by describing their features and benefits. Impart enthusiasm and belief in your products.
Evaluate the ideas and develop the best ones. Identify the appealing aspects of an idea, then list the concerns.	04	**Resolve objections**. Effectively and sensitively resolve the objections that customers inevitably raise.
Summarize the solution. Put together a specific action plan.	05	**Close the deal**. Agree how to move forward with your fulfilment department.

Appealing to buyers

Countless studies have addressed the central questions of sales – why do buyers buy? How do customers make decisions? What do they demand from salespeople? The answers come down to three discernible behaviours: believing in your position, empathy, and trust.

Establishing your position

People buy from people who know their stuff. If the salesperson can't consistently demonstrate that he or she knows what they are talking about, it becomes almost impossible to buy anything from them.

Put yourself in the buying role. You want to buy a new refrigerator, but the salesperson just can't explain why model A is better for you than model B. The chances are that you will shut down as a customer; in fact, you'll probably want to leave and go to a different store. Knowing what you sell inside-out is a given, but your credibility extends far beyond product knowledge. You must become familiar with your customer's business, industry, competitors, and marketplace. You need to be well prepared. It's not hard – almost everything you need to know about your customers and markets is readily available online.

For many buyers, a **salesperson's ability** to **understand** their situation is the single **most compelling reason why** they make the **decision to buy**

Making buying decisions

BELIEVING IN POSITION

EMPATHY

Tip

SET THE TONE
You don't have to be funny in sales, but try to **be fun.** Be the person who **brightens** a room when they enter, rather than the person who brightens up a room when they leave it.

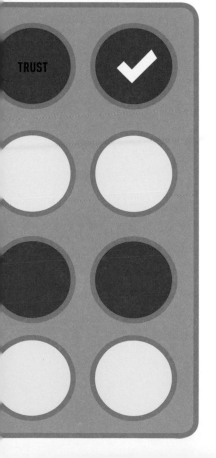

TRUST

Showing empathy

Empathy is the ability to connect with someone – to see things from their perspective. Several recent studies indicate that, for many buyers, a salesperson's ability to understand their situation is the single most compelling reason why they make the decision to buy.

Many people think that empathy depends on similarity of age, background, experience, or point of view. That's a myth. A young salesperson can connect with and relate to someone much more senior if they can identify areas of mutual interest. It's not hard to find common ground. For a start, both are already in the same business – even if they are on different sides of the desk. They may have similar interests and educations: if salespeople allow the customer to talk and genuinely show interest in what they say, the customer will appreciate the empathy they show.

Without understanding the customer and showing real interest in what he or she has to say, a key ingredient in the relationship will be missing. This will mean that the salesperson will remain a mere order taker, at best.

Tip

GET IN TOUCH
Focus on empathy.
Management guru David Maister famously said: "Customers don't care how much you know until they know **how much you care**."

CHECKLIST...
Gaining respect by showing respect

	YES	NO
1 Do you show **respect for your client's space** by, for example, avoiding placing objects on their desk?.....................	☐	☐
2 Do you show **respect for their business** by, for example, asking before you take notes?	☐	☐
3 Do you show **respect for your competitors?** If you put down one of the client's existing suppliers, you are disrespecting the client..	☐	☐

Building trust
Trust takes a long time to build, but only a second to lose. To demonstrate that you can be trusted, you need to be responsive, direct, clear, reliable, and straightforward. Customers don't like to be manipulated and don't appreciate evasiveness. If you get caught being dishonest in any way, you will not only lose that customer, but the ripple effect of your actions will spread far beyond the boundaries of that relationship.

Always assume that your customer is smart and give them due respect: don't play games, make sure to deliver on your promises, and avoid nasty surprises. Follow these simple rules and your customer's trust will follow in time.

65%
of people believe the vital factors in company **reputation** are honest business practices and **trustworthiness**

Becoming credible
You know that you are trustworthy, and your customer thinks you are trustworthy. Good start. Being considered trustworthy and actually being trusted to fulfil a million-dollar contract are two different things. US consulting firm Synectics® Inc. carried out some inspired research that accounts for the difference between these two concepts –it is summarized in the trust formula:

$$trust = \frac{credibility \times intimacy}{risk}$$

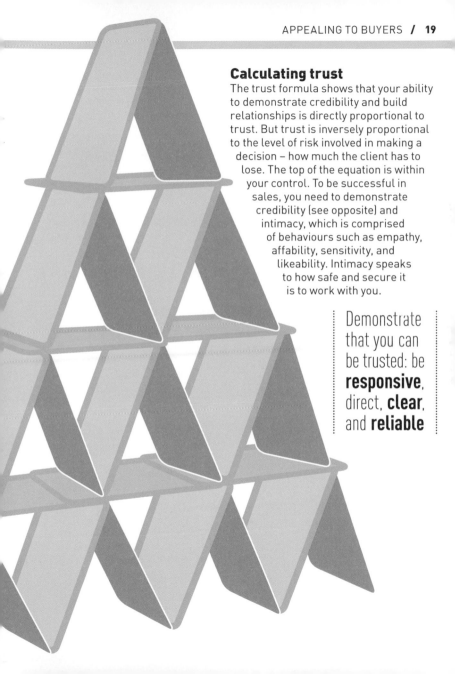

Calculating trust

The trust formula shows that your ability to demonstrate credibility and build relationships is directly proportional to trust. But trust is inversely proportional to the level of risk involved in making a decision – how much the client has to lose. The top of the equation is within your control. To be successful in sales, you need to demonstrate credibility (see opposite) and intimacy, which is comprised of behaviours such as empathy, affability, sensitivity, and likeability. Intimacy speaks to how safe and secure it is to work with you.

> Demonstrate that you can be trusted: be **responsive**, direct, **clear**, and **reliable**

Managing risk

It is the element of risk that is less within your control than credibility or initmacy. Risk works against your ability to build relationships. To be successful, you must effectively learn to manage risk. With that in mind, you, as a salesperson, should constantly ask yourself what

Ways to mitigate risk and build trust

START SMALL

Don't ask for all the business; ask for a piece of it. Show the customer your capabilities and earn the business over time.

IDENTIFY PARALLEL SITUATIONS

Review a similar situation with the customer and demonstrate how it worked previously.

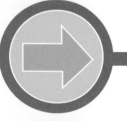

BUILD IN AN EXIT STRATEGY

Let the customer know there will be a way to get out of the situation if things do not work out as planned.

REASSURE THE CUSTOMER

Tell them you'll be there throughout the process; if anything goes awry you'll be ready to take action if necessary.

you can do to make any commitments less risky for the customer. In the 1980s there was a famous marketing adage; "Nobody ever got fired for buying IBM."

That's because the risk was much lower in buying from a well-known organization with a worldwide reputation, than a less-established high-tech company.

GUARANTEE RESULTS
Offer assurance, or at very least, guarantee your commitment to work together with the customer throughout the process.

SHARE THE RISK
Enlighten the customer about the risk for you – if things don't happen as anticipated you'll pay a price as well. Convey that "we're in it together".

TAKE THE BURDEN
Stand behind what you are doing for the customer; let them know you will take full responsibility if things go wrong.

EXPLAIN THE WORST CASE
Make the client aware of all the risks and how you'll do your best to keep them under control.

Differentiating yourself

Whether you're selling computer support, pharmaceuticals, or plumbing supplies, chances are that your competitors offer similar products at equal or better prices with identical back-up. You need to do everything to set your product apart from the others, and there is no better way to differentiate your company than through your approach to your customer.

Adding value

To be a success in sales, you should constantly ask yourself what you can do to add value to the client relationship. If all you do is facilitate the supply of products and services, you are not adding value – just reacting. Even when you are able to provide good solutions to known problems, you are still in reactive mode and are not adding much value. This begins only when you help the customer to determine their needs.

The goal is to move up the value chain and to become a strategic advisor to your customer – someone the customer calls for guidance, ideas, perspective, insights, and, quite simply, help. Once you manage to rise to that level with a customer, your position is rock solid.

Tip
BE FIRST Do whatever you can to keep yourself on the **customer's mind**, by emailing or sending personal notes and letters. Your customers don't think about you as much as you **think about them**, so ensure they think of you first when the **opportunity arises**. But beware – try not to become annoying.

Achieving visibility

Make yourself visible to your customer. To rise to the level of a trusted advisor and differentiate yourself from your competition, try to visit your customers in person on a regular basis. This approach has many benefits: it strengthens the relationship with your customer; it gives you an opportunity to learn about their needs directly and through non-verbal clues; and it enables you to see first hand who your customer regularly interacts with in their organization and the many facets of their work life that remain hidden on the phone.

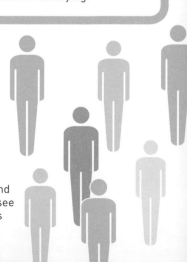

ASK YOURSELF...
Am I "wowing" my customer?   **YES   NO**

1 Are there any relevant **articles** or pieces of
   research that you could send them?... ☐   ☐

2 Can you put them **in touch** with a third party
   who can **provide** something you can't? .... ☐   ☐

3 Do you know of any suppliers who could **help**
   them **reduce their costs**? .... ☐   ☐

4 Can you help them **solve a pressing problem**? .... ☐   ☐

5 Is there a significant **personal event** that you
   could acknowledge?... ☐   ☐

6 Do you know about a **conference or event**
   they may wish to attend? .... ☐   ☐

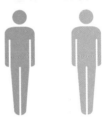

Surprising your customers
Aim to give your customers something
they did not ask for or expect. Let them
know that you care a bit more than
anyone else, that you are willing to do
things others haven't even thought about,
and that you are not just concerned with
getting the sale secured. Tom Peters, the
world-renowned customer-service guru,
talks about delighting customers with
a "WOW!" factor. Showing them you are
different can be what ultimately tips the
scales in your favour when you and your
competitor are running neck and neck.

Understanding
the needs of
customers

Almost every sales professional worth his or her salt acknowledges the key importance of understanding their customers' needs. But what does this really mean, and how do you achieve it in the real world?

26 | IMPLEMENTING THE MODEL

28 | RECOGNIZING NEEDS

34 | PLANNING YOUR APPROACH

36 | MAKING YOUR FIRST MOVE

38 | PRESENTING YOUR CREDENTIALS

40 | HOLDING A SALES MEETING

42 | QUESTIONING FOR NEEDS

48 | LISTENING TO YOUR CLIENT

50 | APPROACHING A PROBLEM

52 | REVIEWING NEEDS

54 | RUNNING A JOINT MEETING

02

Implementing the model

The concept of needs-driven or needs-based selling is nothing new. Corporations have always boasted about their ability to develop products that address their customers' needs, and the concept has been incorporated into sales training programmes for decades. Why then, is needs-based selling often so poorly implemented?

Breaking the 80/20 rule

"Do you understand all of your customers' needs?" In surveys, more that 80 per cent of salespeople answer "yes" to this question. Yet studies of their customers reveal that, seen from the client's side, only 20 per cent of salespeople are addressing needs. Some people refer to this startling discrepancy in perceptions as the "80/20 rule". As a salesperson, you need to understand why this happens, and what you can do to make sure that you're part of the successful 20 per cent.

20%

of **salespeople** are really **addressing needs**, according to their customers

Tip

QUESTION YOURSELF
Think of something you bought recently. Why did you **buy it**? What **need** did you have? How did the product **address** it? How **effective** was the salesperson you bought from? Ask yourself questions like this and your **understanding** of customers' needs will become clearer.

80%

of **salespeople** think they **know** their customers

ASK YOURSELF...
How do I tune in to a client's needs?　　　　**YES　NO**

Each time you interact with a customer, ask yourself these types of questions to put yourself in the right mindset:

1　Do I know **what this person is trying to accomplish?** .... ☐　☐

2　**Am I sure** what they really want from me?..................................... ☐　☐

3　**Have they revealed** their primary concerns?................................. ☐　☐

4　**Have I identified** what's holding them back?................................. ☐　☐

5　**Do I know** what they get from their current supplier?.................... ☐　☐

6　Do I understand **what gaps exist in their current relationship?** ... ☐　☐

7　Have I found out **why are they taking the time to see me?**............. ☐　☐

Taking your time
So why is it that so many salespeople respond in a way that their clients don't want? The answer is – in part – that they are too eager. Early in a sales meeting, they hear a need from a customer and, with the best of intentions, start to address it, start to provide a solution. "Isn't that what needs-driven selling is all about?", you ask. Not exactly: if you hear a need and respond to it immediately, it is a little like reading the first chapter of a book and drawing conclusions regarding the author's message. You know a bit – but just that; the whole story awaits. Any premature recommendation is likely to miss the mark, resulting in a disappointed customer.

Acknowledge that you need to ask **more questions**

Assessing with care
It takes self-confidence to step back, and admit to yourself and your client that you are not ready to make a recommendation yet. You need to acknowledge that you do not fully understand your customer and that you need to ask more questions. This level of humility does not come naturally to most salespeople.

Tip

PRACTISE YOUR SKILLS
When you are in non-business situations with friends or family, **ask yourself** what their needs are relative to your discussion. It helps you become better at **identifying needs** and can make you a **better friend** as well.

Recognizing needs

Before you start questioning your customer to uncover their needs, it helps to know what these needs might look like – and how they are likely to present themselves. You'd be surprised at how even the most seasoned sales professionals have difficulty recognizing needs.

Identifying needs

The respected Harvard economist Theodore Levitt famously said: "People don't want to buy a quarter-inch drill. They want a quarter-inch hole." In other words, people's real needs are sometimes hidden behind apparent solutions. A simple example may help illuminate what Levitt was getting at. Imagine you own a travel agency. A customer walks in days before the winter holidays; he's in a panic because he hasn't arranged that big holiday he promised his wife and children. You listen patiently. He says the family is so excited, but he's worrried that he's left the arrangements too late. He tells you that the holiday is hard to plan because his three children have such different interests – from going to museums to rock climbing – while his wife just needs to have some down time. He brags about how the cost issue is not a big deal to him.

Selling solutions

When salespeople hear stories like this, many immediately start thinking of solutions. "What can we offer him that will address all his issues? If he wants to spend more, let's help him – it's more more commission for us. 'What your family needs, sir, is a spa holiday in Dubai'".

Analyzing all elements

This might indeed be a satisfactory solution, but the salesperson has done little to understand the customer's needs. A little analysis and further questioning might reveal that the client has a need to impress and be respected by his family; to act quickly; to carve out some adult time on his vacation; to have a safe, supervised environment; and many other needs besides. Taking this longer approach has real benefits: the customer feels understood and valued; he'll buy this vacation from you, and come back for your guidance and advice, year after year.

"I know I've left it late, but it has to be something that keeps both my kids and my wife happy."

90%

of **new** consumer products fail because they do not meet the **needs of customers**

Tip

ANALYZE YOUR THOUGHT PROCESS
Whenever you find yourself **offering a solution** to a customer, ask yourself what the **need** is that led to this solution. You'll be amazed at how taking one step back will leave you two steps **forward**.

People's **real needs** are sometimes hidden behind **apparent solutions**

"No problem. Let's start by exploring what you need a little further. What were the best things about your last holiday?"

"Katie and Mike love sports but Jack is much more happy exploring, and Susan just wants to relax."

Reading between the lines

Sometimes your customers will tell you exactly what they need. All you have to do is listen and respond. But if you address only these overt needs, you are not adding much value to the client, and you are doing no more than any of your competitors would do. Where you can differentiate yourself – and win the client's respect and trust – is by hearing and responding to implied needs. So your task is to look for the needs behind what the customer is saying. For example, if the client complains about his boss constantly second guessing him, he may be expressing a need to have a solid, tightly reasoned explanation for his buying decisions. Successful sales professionals know how to uncover these implicit needs – indeed, it is what drives their long-term success.

Tip

RECOGNIZE MOTIVES
Look out for **customers** who are risk averse, or who seem to worry about how they are going to **appear**; they tend to be driven more by **personal needs**.

7% of **information** given only in words is **absorbed**

Accounting for feelings

Selling would be a far easier task if customers could be relied on always to buy for sound business reasons – such as return on investment, quality, value, and competence. If the buyer always made his or her decision dispassionately, rather than based on how that decision made them feel, then reading their requirements would be straightforward.

You can **differentiate** yourself – and win the client's **respect** and **trust** – by **hearing** and **responding to implied needs**. Look for **the needs** behind what the customer says

Business and personal needs

Business needs are measurable while personal needs are subjective. Below are some examples of each to illustrate the differences between the two.

BUSINESS NEEDS	PERSONAL NEEDS
Reduce cost	**Look good** in front of peers
Increase efficiency	**Gain** recognition
Shorten production time	**Get** that promotion
Become more effective	**Minimize** the risk
Increase profitability	**Boost** personal status
Improve turnaround time	**Decrease** stress

Empathizing with clients

All customers – however company-focused they may be – are to some extent influenced by their individual and personal needs. These needs delve into areas that are harder to quantify – security, connecting with others, ego, and comfort. For this reason, showing empathy with the customer will bring you rich rewards.

Tip

BE SENSITIVE
After **each meeting**, ask yourself what the **customer** didn't say. You'll probably **unearth** some needs they did not consciously know they had.

How to find out client needs

71%

of customers **value and use the businesses** that can show they know **customer expectations** and try to **anticipate their needs**

Introduce and open the questioning session

Ask the right questions

Beginning the questioning

Before you begin to question your client to determine their needs, let them know why you need the information, how it will benefit them, and how it relates to the agenda. Explain that by answering your questions they will:

● Help you focus on the right issues
● Allow you to make better recommendations
● Get an opportunity to outline their concerns
● Ensure that you learn about them. They are more likely to be open and honest with their answers if they understand the structure of the needs determination process (see above).

Research on the **selling process** points to one **conclusion**: the **more** questions you **ask** your client, the more success you'll enjoy

Tip

SELLING BLANKS
Approach some **sales calls** as if you were "selling without a product." This forces you to **focus strictly** on the customer – a productive habit to get into.

Case study

NEW BLOOD FOR CITIBANK
In the early 1980s, Citibank was one of the first major financial organizations to attempt the creation of a unique sales culture. The Consumer Banking Group interviewed many of the largest sales training companies, but – to the surprise of many – hired a young, small and virtually unknown firm to lead the charge. When the decision-maker was asked why she chose that firm, her response was simple: "Of all the firms we interviewed, they did the best job of demonstrating that they understood our needs. And if that's what we want to teach our people, let's go with people who practise what they preach." Enough said.

Listen for the needs

Review and check the needs

50%
of **customers** leave their **existing** suppliers to **work** with other companies within a period of **five years**

Asking, and asking again
Many pieces of research on the selling process point to one simple conclusion: the more questions you ask of your client, the more success you'll enjoy – the person who understands the most needs is primed to win the business. But the corollary is that the longer you manage a relationship, the more likely you are to lose sales. That is because, over time, you become complacent, making assumptions about the customer rather than asking questions. That's why many salespeople report a falling share of sales, just when they thought the relationship was thriving. So you need to keep asking questions consistently, methodically, and creatively.

Planning your approach

Most sales managers agree that the margins separating good, very good, and excellent salespeople are not dependent upon what happens face-to-face, but what happens before and after the sales process. You may feel energized and ready to jump straight into a sales meeting with a new customer, but if you spend time planning the content and thinking through the process, your chances of success will be greatly enhanced.

Doing your homework

The first part of planning is getting your content right – ensuring that you have all the information you need for every stage of the entire sales process.

Start your preparation by determining the objectives of the meeting, both for you and for the customer. Once these aims are established, ask yourself what you already know about the customer and what you still need to learn.

Researching thoroughly

There is no excuse for not knowing what is going on in your customer's industry and marketplace. There are numerous sources of data that you can access online to make sure you are prepared, including – but not limited to – annual reports, product brochures, articles, industry magazines, and trade show summaries. Check your customer's website and try to discover what changes

Planning your approach with questions

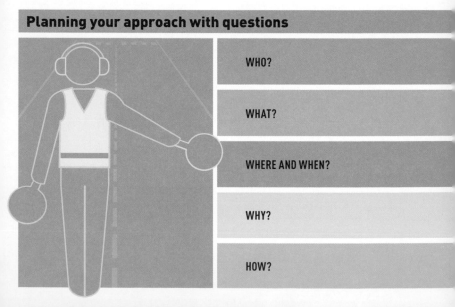

WHO?

WHAT?

WHERE AND WHEN?

WHY?

HOW?

are on the horizon in their business. Find out about their competitors, see what the marketplace is saying, and understand what your customers are demanding.

If appropriate, think about what you want to recommend to the customer, and the corresponding features and benefits. Try to anticipate objections, and identify what the real issues might be and what answers you may be able to provide.

74%
of clients **trusted** salespeople with **industry** knowledge

Preparing the process
Getting the content right is important, but you also need to plan how to manage the selling process – the way you deliver the information. Consider all the stages of the selling process, from opening the meeting to closing the deal. Do you know what you will do and say at each stage and how you will manage the transitions between the phases?

Rehearsing well
Feeling relaxed and well prepared is crucial, so rehearse your presentation repeatedly, and ask for feedback from colleagues. Practise delivering your questions, resolving objections, and even closing. This will highlight any areas in which you are less than confident, and reveal any holes in the information you need to succeed.

O **Who** makes the decisions?
O **Who** should I see?

O **Who** will do what from our side?

O **What** questions will I ask?
O **What** drives this customer's decisions?

O **What** ideas will I suggest?
O **What** objections do I anticipate?

O **Where** is the best place to conduct the meeting?

O **When** would be the most effective time?

O **Why** is this approach good for our business?

O **Why** are we targeting this specific customer?

O **How** will I run the meeting?

O **How** can I differentiate us from our competitors?

Making your first move

It has lots of names – the initial contact, the cold call, the first call, the canvas, the exploratory call, and others. That first visit to a prospective customer can be a daunting, even scary, experience for most people early in their careers. The good news is that this does change over time.

Finding the way in

You can't set up a first meeting until you have a lead. Experiment with finding different sources of leads:

- Former customers
- Referrals from existing customers
- Newspaper articles and trade and industry publications
- Trade shows/symposiums
- Online business articles and social media contacts
- Centres of influence (third parties).

Armed with leads, your key prospecting tool will be a well-written email. You will need to send three key emails during the prospecting process; one to introduce yourself, one to confirm an appointment to meet, and one to follow up the initial meeting. You may wish to try a traditional letter for the initial approach – it will set you apart from the competition.

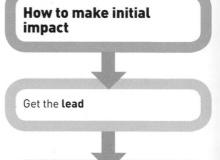

How to make initial impact

Get the **lead**

Make the **call** and **secure an appointment**

Making an appointment

In some industries, it can be acceptable just to drop by and ask to see someone, but regardless of the business you are in, you will be more successful if you obtain an appointment first. Send a confirmation email, letting the customer know that you are looking forward to meeting them and confirm the date, time, and time allocation. Review your own agenda and attach some relevant material for the customer to look at in advance. Encourage them to invite anyone else from their organization who might benefit from attending.

MAKING THE FIRST VISIT

Dos	Don'ts
O Confirming the meeting in writing to show interest	O Just showing up without putting in the preparation time
O Being humble – you haven't been there before	O Showing unfounded familiarity – it's only the first meeting
O Doing your homework and demonstrating what you have learned in preparation for the visit	O Treating this meeting as if it were just another meeting
O Showing appreciation for the customer taking the meeting	O Acting as though you are entitled to be there
O Asking lots of questions of the customer and letting them talk	O Presenting specific recommendations

Write a **formal email** to introduce yourself and your organization

⬇

Confirm the appointment in an email

⬇

Send a **follow-up** email

⬇

Make the **initial visit**

Creating an impression

Your first meeting with a new prospect may have many purposes – from a simple introduction to a full-blown sales call. Whatever the reason, stay calm and begin the process of understanding your potential customer's needs. You do not have to be specific at this stage (although you should be prepared to present your company's credentials – see pp.38–39). Instead, establish rapport, and let the customer do most of the talking.

Learn what you can about the individual and their business. Look for, and reinforce, common ground. Are they familiar with your company? Is there any relevant history between your organizations that could form a bond? Do you share interests or acquaintances in the industry?

Learn about the **individual** and their **business**

Presenting your credentials

Despite your best intentions to focus on the customer's needs, you will often find that you are asked to give a quick explanation of who you are and what you have to offer – a credentials presentation – before the customer will give you any information about themselves.

Aiming for needs first

A credentials presentation is an overview of your company, what it does, and how it adds value to its customers. You need to be prepared to give a brief presentation, but if you can avoid having to do so at this early stage of your relationship with a new customer, you should: as soon as you start talking about how to help them before identifying and confirming their needs, it becomes more about you than about them. If your customer says to you: "Tell me about your company", it can sometimes work to respond with: "I'll be delighted to explain who we are and how we may be of assistance, but I can do that much more effectively if I learn a bit about you first." If the customer agrees, you can start the needs-determination process; if not, you will have to make a credentials presentation.

98%

of people only buy after **trust** has been built, not at a **first** meeting

"Our **products** address a **range of needs**"

Give some **history** about the company and yourself

Tip

KEEP IT GENERAL
Use the **presentation** to give a brief **overview of needs** you can **fulfil** and your product line. Don't make assumptions about your customer's needs and don't offer a particular product or service.

Getting the message right

A good way to build a credentials presentation is to use your team – not just the sales team, but anyone in the business who would like to contribute. Ask different members of the team to put themselves in the position of a customer of your company, and talk to you about what they would like to hear. As you build your presentation, practise it with the team: discuss how it sounds and refine it until you get it right.

The key to making a successful credentials presentation is to keep it short, focused, and to the point. Don't overload the customer with information – you will (hopefully) have the opportunity to do that later. Give some history about the company and yourself as a way to explain who you are. If you have an interesting anecdote about how the company started, don't be afraid to share it. Aim to tell them the kinds of things you do and the kinds of companies you work with, and briefly outline your success stories. Discuss needs generally, and then explain why what you have to offer can be of value to a company like theirs. Again, words like "can", "could", or "might" are more appropriate as you have not yet learned enough about your customer to get specific.

A **credentials presentation** is an **overview** of your company, what it does, and how it **adds value** to its customers

CHECKLIST...
Preparing a credentials presentation

		YES	NO
1	Have you **discussed** with your team how you want to position your company to people who aren't familiar with what you do?.....................................	☐	☐
2	Have you used your company's **mission and vision statements** to provide key facts and figures?	☐	☐
3	Have you trimmed your presentation so that it can be **delivered within a few minutes?**............................	☐	☐
4	Have you **practised** in front of a friend or colleague until you are **fully confident** in your delivery?................................	☐	☐

Holding a sales meeting

When you make an appointment to see a client – whether it is your first or your fiftieth – you are effectively calling a meeting for that customer. For the meeting to run well, you need to take the initiative, while at the same time acknowledging that the meeting belongs to the customer – it must be focused on providing solutions to their problems.

Building rapport

What happens in the first few minutes of a sales visit sets the tone for the entire meeting. It helps to break the opening down into three critical steps: building rapport, confirming the agenda, and moving into the meeting itself.

At the start of the meeting, make sure everyone is comfortable, knows who is who, and has a chance to connect informally. Encourage small talk or a discussion about general business conditions. Use your intuition to decide when to move on – you need to work at your customer's comfort level, not your own. Here are a few ideas to help you get the conversation off to a good start:

- Look around the client's office for something to trigger conversation, such as a picture or trophy.
- Compliment the customer on their office or facility – but be sincere.
- Thank the customer for their time.
- Discuss something you know about their business – a relevant news event, for example – to show that you've done your homework.

79%

of people think a **meeting** has more customer **impact** than phone or email contact

Setting the agenda

Next, you should ensure that everyone is clear about the objectives of the meeting. Even though this is a sales call, it requires a clear agenda, distributed in advance, that takes into account your needs and your client's (remember, it is their meeting). Give each person the opportunity to express their interest in the meeting and what they would like to get out of it. This is crucial: you may not realize the status or position of a participant in your meeting, and run the risk of missing out on a huge opportunity.

Finally, confirm the amount of time available for the meeting, and stick to it. Customers resent people who overstay their welcome.

Guiding the meeting

Old-style salespeople were loath to lose control of a meeting, and so did all the talking and tried to force the customer on to their agenda. This style isn't consistent with a problem-solving approach to selling. Instead, you should acknowledge that the meeting belongs to the customer – you are there to solve their problems, after all. Your role is more as facilitator, you need to ensure that the meeting runs smoothly. Once you begin addressing issues on the agenda, ensure that the meeting stays focused on the stated purposes. Try to draw out ideas from all participants, then move the meeting towards an action plan, and schedule the follow-up.

Roles in the sales meeting

THE SALESPERSON
O **Facilitates** the sales meeting
O May take **minutes**
O Participates in **finding solutions**

THE CLIENT
O **Owns** the problem
O May **chair** the meeting
O Participates in **finding solutions**

OTHER PARTICIPANTS
O **Participate** in finding good solutions
O Contribute **problem-solving** resources

Questioning for needs

Of all the skills demanded of a successful salesperson, questioning remains the most important. This is simply because you can't hope to understand a customer's needs without asking questions in a thoughtful, credible, and sensitive way.

Running the session

When you question a customer at a sales meeting, you need to keep the session light – think of it as an open discussion rather than an interrogation. Customers who are comfortable invariably reveal more – and more useful – information.

The questions you ask to determine needs fall into three broad categories – fact-finding questions, needs-oriented questions, and big-picture questions – each of which are considered below. There are no hard-and-fast rules about the types of question you should ask your customer, but experience suggests that a ratio of around five fact-finding questions, to three needs-oriented questions, and one big-picture question is comfortable for the client and achievable for you.

A ratio of around **five fact-finding** questions, to **three needs-oriented** questions, and **one big-picture question** is comfortable for the **client** and achievable for you

Finding the facts

To scope out an account or manage a relationship, you need some fundamental pieces of information about the client – their company structure; number of employees; their customers, partners, suppliers; and so on. These questions may seem obvious, but it's surprising how often they are overlooked. The aim of the questions is to elicit information, so they tend not to be imaginative (virtually everybody asks them). Most can be answered "yes" or "no" or with a fact. But some questions may be quite provocative, for example, "Who makes the decisions here?" Questions are essential, but will not do much to differentiate you from your competition.

61%

of salespeople surveyed said they were **confident** about **discovering customer needs** and problems. These salespeople were **28%** more likely to achieve their **targets**

Tip

LEARN FROM THE PROS
Watch the **great interviewers** on television. They ask **short questions** and don't give the person being interviewed possible answers. They ask a question and stop talking; try the same **technique**.

Examining needs

Needs-oriented questions get the customer talking and are far more open-ended. The questions can be quite imaginative – "If you could change one thing about the way you do business today, what would that be?" – or even provocative. Typically, these questions do not have "right" or "wrong" answers; they open up new areas of discussion, and will absolutely help to differentiate you from your competition.

Responses from the customer will encompass everything from their objectives, goals, hopes, expectations, and aspirations to their problems, concerns, worries, and fears. As your relationship with the client evolves, you can ask progressively deeper questions that will help reinforce trust.

Tip

BEWARE OF THE WHY?
Be careful of **questions** that begin with a **"why"** – they can appear judgemental and condescending and can put people on the defensive. It helps to **introduce** these types of questions with a preamble.

Exploring the big picture

Big-picture questions position you to uncover needs that the customer does not necessarily know he or she has. They are strategic in nature, in essence asking the customer to think about things that they may not like to consider – the future of the business, difficulties to be overcome, the need to plan, contingencies, and long-term goals. Big-picture questions require planning on your part because they can lead to uncomfortable – albeit valuable – discussions. They are necessarily thought-provoking, and will stay in the customer's mind for a long time. They elevate the conversation, and will eventually result in your being perceived as an advisor or consultant – much more than a salesperson.

Big-picture questions position you to **uncover needs** that the **customer** does not necessarily know he or she has

Big-picture questions require planning

Case study

ASKING THE RIGHT QUESTIONS

One of the classic stories in the sales business recalls how Pepsi Cola won the airline business from Coca Cola in the 1990s. At the time, Coca Cola owned the in-flight business and there was no way Pepsi could win the business in a price war. The new national sales manager of Pepsi was about to make his first call on one of the airlines and had prepared a lavish and thoughtful presentation. At the last minute, one of his internal resources suggested that they show up with only a pad and pen – no presentation at all.

Against his better instincts, the Pepsi manager agreed. For two hours, all they did was ask questions and learn about the airline. They hardly mentioned Pepsi. But they learned that beyond ensuring safety, the biggest need the airline had was to sell more tickets. They had uncovered a critical need that they had to meet if they were to be successful in their bid for the business.

They developed a plan to give retailers coupons that allowed them to buy airline tickets at a discount: at the time, this was a unique approach that departed from the pattern of typical promotions. The airlines loved the idea, awarded Pepsi the business, and generated millions of dollars worth of extra sales within a year. A legendary result.

They are **thought-provoking**, and will stay in the **customer's mind**

They **elevate** the **conversation**, and will result in your being perceived as an **advisor** or **consultant**

Planning the discussion

Most people are naturally suspicious of questions. When determining needs, you should be as sensitive as possible during the process of questioning your client.

- Give a preamble: let the customer know that questions are coming, why you are asking, and how it is in their interests to answer.
- Cluster questions into categories, focusing on strategy, finance, inventory, and so on, each with its own preamble.
- Be straightforward in your questions.
- Do not shy away from asking all the tough questions.

82%

of **business leaders** in a **global survey** felt they were **better understood** after a meeting, and **54%** agreed that **personal meetings** were essential to **gauge focus and engagement** from colleagues and **customers**

Questions to investigate the client's needs

FACT FINDING

- O What are your **annual sales**?
- O Who are your **current suppliers**?
- O **How often** do you purchase?
- O How much do you **spend** on this account?
- O Who makes the **decisions**?

NEEDS ORIENTED

- O What are your **expectations** of someone like me?
- O What changes are you **initiating** to stay competitive?
- O How has **globalization** impacted your business?
- O What are some of the **biggest challenges** you face today?
- O How has your **customer base** changed?

BIG PICTURE

- O What is your **vision** for the company?
- O Where would you like the company to be **in five years**?
- O What obstacles could prevent that from **happening**?
- O How do you see yourself **leveraging your strengths** in the long term?
- O How will you ensure that you **benefit from globalization**?

Listening to your client

You can ask your client brilliantly incisive questions to determine their needs. But these are worth little if you don't listen to their responses. Listening isn't easy – studies reveal that we retain a tiny percentage of what we hear – but it is a critical skill for any salesperson.

Keeping tuned in

As a salesperson, you are the eyes and ears of your organization; what you learn about your client in a sales meeting will make your company stand or fall. You should be listening at a high level all the time – collecting facts, information, and business-related concepts – but most of all, listening for needs.

> What you **learn** about your client in a **sales meeting** will make your **company stand** or fall

Overcoming obstacles

Of course, this is the ideal scenario, and in reality your ability to listen is jeopardized by many factors. Instead of listening, you may start anticipating the next question, planning your response, or trying to understand what the customer meant. You may become distracted by thinking about your route home or your meetings tomorrow. Attentive listening is often harder than it seems, because we think much faster than we can talk. Whatever your reason for tuning out of a business conversation, you are sure to miss some vital details.

> **Tip**
>
> **ASK FIRST**
> Always ask if it's **OK to make notes** and show **respect for confidentiality**. Clients will rarely decline and will probably be **flattered** that you want to record what they say.

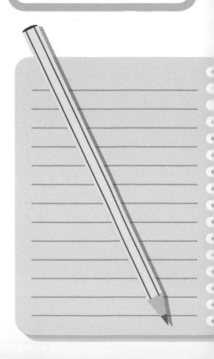

SHOWING INTEREST

Four out of five clients think that when you don't make notes, you aren't fully engaged. This research is borne out by a story related by a sales manager, who, along with a colleague, began a sales meeting with a prospective client. Neither was taking notes. After a few awkward minutes, the client called his assistant on the phone and said: "Please bring two pads and two pens for our guests as I would like to have the impression that they are at least somewhat interested in what I have to say." This is a true story – don't let this happen to you!

Mastering active learning

There are many ways to enhance your listening skills, of which one of the best known is Active Listening. This concept has been around more than half a century and describes a structured form of listening that focuses attention on the speaker. A listener consciously attends fully to the speaker and then repeats, in their own words, what they think the speaker has said, often interpreting the words in terms of feelings.

Making notes

A simple, and arguably more effective technique can be set out in just two words – Take Notes, or more accurately, Make Notes. From the minute the customer starts talking, you should put pen to paper. The distinction between "making" and "taking" notes is important because you are also jotting down any connections you make, and capturing on paper the need, the concern, the issue, the opportunity. Don't analyze too much – there will be time for that later.

The discipline of making notes has further benefits – it stops you from trying to respond too early, and it ensures that you listen to the customer throughout the meeting – it's a fact that many people "save the best for last", revealing their deepest needs towards the end of a conversation. If you present too early, chances are you will miss hearing crucial information.

75% of customers said they chose to **buy from** salespeople who **listened** to them

Approaching a problem

Bringing a problem-solving approach into your dealings with customers has clear benefits. But how do you put it into practice? Problem-solving seems intangible and difficult, but following a structured process, such as the technique of brainstorming, will bring focus to your interactions with customers and increase your chances of sales success.

Setting the scene

Problem solving requires creativity – but that doesn't mean chaos. When you bring together a group to develop creative solutions, you need to give the meeting structure. Be sure to define the task, decide what approach you will use and how much time is available, and establish who is chairing, facilitating, and minuting the meeting.

Next, the group should identify the problem and set it into a proper context of background information. Why is the problem a problem? Could it be turned into an opportunity? Has the problem been addressed before, and how? Who is responsible for results? Once the meeting has been staged and the problem defined, the group is ideally positioned to generate good ideas through brainstorming.

Encouraging creative solutions

When you begin a brainstorming session, invite ideas, perspectives, recommendations, and new insights. Encourage participants to be speculative and open to ideas – the meeting should be energetic, exciting, and fun. Resist any temptation to evaluate ideas as soon as they are put forward – anything goes. The opportunity to be innovative invariably yields richer results than if individuals feel constrained by rules or limitations.

> **Tip**
>
> **MAKE SPACE FOR INNOVATION**
> Don't **overdefine** a problem. Usually, if people **learn** too much about a problem, they will become less willing to **speculate** and will find themselves putting on the same blinkers as the person with the problem.

80%

of people think that **unlocking creativity** is a **vital factor** for **worldwide** economic **growth**

In focus

BRAINSTORMING
When it is done right, the technique of brainstorming taps people's capacity for lateral thinking and free association and boosts creative output. The concept was conceived in the 1920s by Alex Osborn, partner in international advertising agency BBDO (he was the "O" in the company). Osborn summarized the technique in the statement: "It is easier to tone down a wild idea than to think up a new one." Many precede their brainstorming sessions with creativity or relaxation exercises to help participants move into a more creative state.

Encourage participants to be **speculative and open** – the meeting should be **energetic, exciting, and fun**

Evaluating results
Brainstorming is a great way to spend the first half of a problem- solving session. The second part must be devoted to selecting the most exciting ideas and evaluating them diligently to develop solutions.

The evaluation process doesn't have to be complex, but it does have to be managed with care. Once an idea has been selected, the challenge becomes how to turn it into a solution.

Discovering the positive
One of the most common approaches suggests first identifying the appealing aspects of an idea and then listing concerns. Identifying the positives ensures that the parts of the idea that you want to save are captured and preserved. Then address each concern, beginning with the most troubling, until the idea becomes acceptable. At this point, when the idea has been transformed into a solution, carefully summarize your conclusions and put together a specific action plan that includes the next steps to implement the results.

Reviewing needs

The perfect way to complete the needs assessment and move into the presentation phase is to demonstrate to the customer that you have been listening, that you understand what they have been saying, and that you're in tune with what they hope to accomplish.

Selling before presenting

Everything you have done up to this point has been focused on learning the needs of your customer. But before you start to present your solutions, you should demonstrate a clear understanding of his or her situation. If you review the needs well, you'll demonstate credibility, empathy, sensitivity, and trustworthiness – and many customers will make their decision to buy from you at this point, even before you have presented your range of goods and services. Conversely, without thoroughly reviewing the needs, you risk misunderstanding your client and missing the mark with your recommendations.

Tip

SEEK CONFIRMATION
If there are **several people** in the room, check with each of them that your understanding of the **needs** matches theirs. Just because one person **agrees** with you doesn't mean they all do.

82%

of **top** salespeople are **inquisitive**: they show interest and ask questions

In focus

THE PSYCHOLOGY OF LISTENING

Carl Rogers (1902–1987) was one of the world's greatest psychologists and students of human communication. He famously said that the "greatest compliment one human being can pay another is to demonstrate that he was listening." When a sales professional takes the time to review with a customer his or her understanding of that customer's needs, they are indeed paying the client a great compliment and differentiating themselves – yet again – from the competition in an emphatic manner.

CHOOSING YOUR WORDS

Dos	Don'ts
O **"Here's my understanding of what you said..."**	O "What you need is..."
O **"I may be reading too much into this, but it appears that..."**	O "You said that..."
O **"How I interpreted X's statement was that you had a desire to..."**	O "X told us that you wanted..."

Ensuring a close match

When you begin the review, choose your words carefully: tell the client what you heard as opposed to what they said. The distinction is subtle, but avoids putting words in the client's mouth (see box, above). Start by summarizing the client's overt needs and move to those you need to infer. Ask the client to confirm that your review is correct, and ask them to prioritize their needs. Ask if you missed anything, if there's anything they'd like to add, or if your understanding is flawed. You just might pick up another need along the way.

Timing the review

The best time to review needs is either at the end of a needs-determination meeting or at the beginning of a meeting in which you are presenting (especially if new people are present, or a lot of time has passed since the last meeting). Concluding a meeting by reviewing needs ends it on a positive note and sets the stage for the next meeting, when you will be presenting. If you have done everything right, the client will already have a strong inclination to buy from you.

Tell the client **what you heard** as **opposed** to what **they said**. The **distinction** is subtle

Start by summarizing the client's **overt needs** and **move** to those you need **to infer**

Running a joint meeting

Bringing a colleague with you – whether it's your manager, a subject expert, another member of the team, or the new salesperson who recently joined the company – can potentially make your sales meeting much more effective. However, joint sales meetings need to be managed carefully if they are to live up to their potential.

Being prepared

Preparation is the key to effective joint sales meetings. Firstly, anyone you bring with you to the meeting needs to have a full understanding of its objective. At the very least, they need to know who the customer is, what they do, where you are in the relationship, and what you hope to accomplish. Equally importantly, your colleagues need to be clear about what their role in the meeting will be, or you run the risk that they will be unprepared. Are they there to ask questions, make recommendations, help deal with objections, or just to demonstrate support and interest?

> **Tip**
>
> **TALK UP YOUR COLLEAGUES**
> When you **introduce** your colleagues on a joint call, **emphasize** why it is so **important** that they have been able to come along. For example: "I'm delighted Susan could join us – she has been working on these kinds of problems for 15 years."

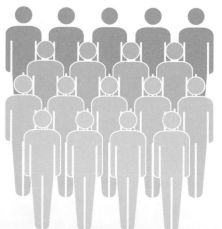

Managing a joint meeting

In a joint sales meeting, it is even more important that you act as the facilitator, managing the process and trying to ensure that the meeting fulfils both your own objectives and your customer's. Get the meeting off to a positive start by inviting introductions: make sure that everyone knows who everyone else is, and that they are clear about what each party hopes to accomplish. During the meeting, it is important that every member of your team makes a contribution, so call on your colleagues when their expertise is needed, and explain why: "I would like John to answer that question as it falls within his area of expertise".

Benefits of joint sales meetings

SPECIALIST KNOWLEDGE

Inviting colleagues from different functional areas of your organization to join you at the meeting allows you to offer a **greater range of expertise** to the customer.

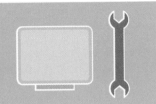

TWO PAIRS OF EARS

Sales meetings can be **fast paced**, especially if you are acting as the facilitator. If you have a colleague with you, they can **pick up** on small details that you may miss.

IMPROVING PERFORMANCE

Your colleagues can give you **feedback** on your performance, enabling you to be even **more effective** at your next sales meeting.

DIFFERENT PERSPECTIVES

With more than one of you **interpreting** what the customer is saying, you may get a **fuller understanding** of the customer's needs.

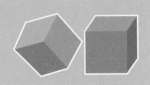

LOOKING GOOD

Bringing a team – especially if it includes **senior members** of your organization – may **impress** the customer, and make them feel that they are **important** to you.

Recommending
solutions

Providing solutions and making recommendations is the part of the selling process that most salespeople like best. It's time to demonstrate how you can help the customer, to tell your story, and present your products and services.

58 | USING FEATURES AND BENEFITS

60 | TARGETING THE PITCH

62 | OFFERING YOUR IDEAS

64 | ASKING FOR FEEDBACK

03

Using features and benefits

Client presentations take many forms; they range from informal one-to-one meetings to formal expositions to a conference room full of potential clients. Surprisingly, regardless of the situation, your approach will not vary that much: your presentation will focus on features and benefits.

Defining the terms

Salespeople have used features and benefits to describe their products and services for many decades. This approach has stood the test of time for one reason – it works!

Features tell customers how products or services work. They are characteristics, descriptions, attributes, specifications, and explanations. Benefits explain how the product helps – why it is important to the client and how it addresses their needs. Benefits set out to the customer the value of the item being discussed and why it is in their interests to purchase it.

61%

of customers will **research** products before **they decide** to **buy anything**

Linking features and benefits

FEATURES OF PRODUCT

O Neat design
O Solid construction
O Ergonomic features
O Reinforced materials

Explaining features

People make the decision to buy things because of their benefits rather than their features. However, most salespeople are more comfortable talking about features than benefits. It's not hard to see why. Features are facts and hard to debate. You will rarely be challenged when you explain the features of a product or service – they are tangible and objectively notable.

Selling the benefits

Benefits, on the other hand, are educated guesses. They are usually subjective – what might be a benefit for one person may not be a benefit for another. Talking about benefits makes some people uncomfortable because it feels like a "hard sell". It shouldn't. Benefits do no more than explain why a recommendation makes sense.

Making benefit statements

When you make your presentation, think in terms of benefit statements, and always try to link the features of your product or service to the benefits. If you do not you are only telling half the story. The example below shows the difference in the types of statement a salesperson may make to highlight benefits from the features of certain products.

Features tell customers how **products or services work**. **Benefits** explain **how the product helps** – why it is **important** to the client and how it **addresses their needs**

BENEFITS OF PRODUCT

O Saves space, so adds convenience

O Durable – has a long lifespan, saving money

O Enhanced performance, comfort for user

O Easy to carry and robust, gives more flexibility

Targeting the pitch

Features and benefits are the trusted selling tools that address the client's questions "What?" and "So what?" But if you can answer one further question – "What's in it for me?" – you'll set yourself apart from the competition. This question addresses the specific benefit – the particular needs of an individual customer.

Focusing on specifics

Your ability to express the features and benefits of your products is vital, but there's one more conceptual step to take – understanding and presenting specific benefits. Every customer buys for slightly different reasons: some base their decisions on quality, convenience, and price; others on the level of service, or personal reasons that reflect how they feel about themselves. Specific benefits speak to the confirmed, most important, needs of a particular client; they differ from generic benefits, which make broader statements about the value of a product or service.

Prioritizing your messages

Information about your products and services and their corresponding features and benefits is fixed information – it's what you might include in your brochure, website, or catalogue. In contrast, the needs of each customer and the specific benefits you present are variable. This variable information is at the heart of the needs-driven selling process – it's what elevates your presentation far above the canned pitch.

Starting with unique benefits

So, when the time comes to present, deliver the variable information first. Start by succinctly reviewing all the customer's needs; next, try to make recommendations and demonstrate how they address the customer's needs – the specific benefits. Only when this is done should you move on to presenting the generic features and benefits. At first glance, this ordering of the information appears back-to-front – going from the specific to the general. However, it addresses the reality of your audience's attention span. High-level listening efficiency lasts a frighteningly short time – up to 90 seconds – before dipping precipitously. Specific benefits are what close deals, so be sure to get them in early, before your client's attention wanders.

Tip

HOLD BACK THE BROCHURE

Try using your **sales brochure** only after you have presented, not before. **Highlight** the areas where your products meet the client's needs.

Specific benefits close deals, so get them in **early**

THE HUMAN TOUCH
Back in the 1960s, social forecasters were predicting that salespeople would be made obsolete by the turn of the century through advances in computing and revolutionary marketing vehicles, such as direct mail and telemarketing. They could not have been more wrong. More people are selling today than ever before, and even professions that never considered using the "s" word in the past, such as banking, accounting, law, and medicine, find themselves soliciting business on a day-to-day basis. That's because the consumer does not want to buy from a catalogue, a piece of mail, or a voice on the telephone. They want to buy from a person who listens to them, understands their needs, and responds with appropriate products and services.

Ordering your pitch

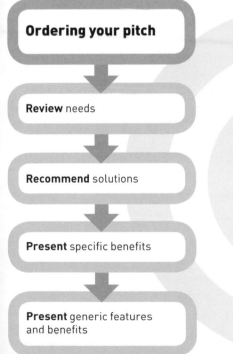

Review needs

Recommend solutions

Present specific benefits

Present generic features and benefits

Offering your ideas

Many sales professionals think that all they have to offer is their products and services. But it's not just what's in your bag that's important – it's what's in your head. When you present your customer with an idea that helps them do their job a bit better, teaches them something new, or addresses a personal issue, you are building value in your relationship that lets you leapfrog way ahead of your competitors.

Giving to receive

An uncompensated idea has no revenue attached to it. When a sales professional presents a customer with an uncompensated idea he or she surprises the customer with novel and unexpected thinking that accumulates great value and brings long-term financial reward. If you're prepared to give, you will probably receive.

> Let them **know** you have been **thinking** about their situation and that **you have an idea** for them

ASK YOURSELF...
About offering new ideas

YES NO

Before each client meeting, think of areas in which you could help the client by offering uncompensated ideas:

1 Are they doing something that we know they could do better with **better technology** or software? .... ☐ ☐

2 Are there problems that they **consistently** raise, and can I **research** solutions? .... ☐ ☐

3 Is there something in the client's non-working life where I could **offer an idea** – for example, suggesting a venue for their child's party? .... ☐ ☐

4 Is there something about the client's facility that could be **improved** – a lack of signage, for example? .... ☐ ☐

5 Can I enhance the client's **industry knowledge** – by recommending a good seminar or training programme? .... ☐ ☐

Case study

GOING THE EXTRA MILE

A US training company was seeking bids for a new video system. They spoke to three potential suppliers, each of whom made good recommendations. There was little to choose between the three companies on price, quality, capabilities, and service agreements. While they were in the decision-making process, the salesperson from one of the three suppliers emailed an article that appeared in *The Wall Street Journal* that day about one of the training company's clients. The email was accompanied by a short note: "I'm sure you saw this, but just in case...". Without any other differentiators, the salesperson who took the extra step won the contract.

Proposing new offers

Salespeople are reluctant to present uncompensated ideas for fear that they will come across as inappropriate or embarrassing. So is it really worth taking the risk of crossing established boundaries? The answer is an emphatic "yes". When the customer sees that you have put in effort to offer a new perspective they will know that you value the relationship – even if they are not keen on the idea itself.

Adding value

The idea you offer up doesn't have to be related to business and it doesn't need to be Earth-shattering; however, it must add value – don't present an idea just for the sake of doing so. Your customer doesn't know that you're about to offer an uncompensated idea, so before starting, get their permission. Let them know you have been thinking about their situation and that you have an idea for them. Ask if they think it's appropriate for you to present it. Most customers will be intrigued. Next, express what you think their need is, present the idea, and explain its specific benefits. Be humble when you offer the idea and give credit to others whenever you can; there's nothing to be gained by trying to make the customer think that you're smarter than they are.

Tip

TIME YOUR TIPS

Uncompensated ideas are best unveiled at the end of the meeting, not the beginning. They offer a **great way** to end any meeting on a **high note**.

20%

of customers take **one year** to make a purchase

Asking for feedback

You have delivered your presentation. Your customers nodded enthusiastically throughout, so your recommendations must have been spot on. Or so you think. The only way to be sure and to move to the next stage of the selling process is to ask your client for feedback. It's time to hear from them.

Facing the music

Even seasoned salespeople will hesitate before asking the customer to respond to their recommendations. A lot of time went into getting to this point and the fear of rejection can be paralyzing. No matter how many times you tell yourself that it is not you that's being rejected but your product or idea, it's hard not to take it personally. But don't make the mistake of delivering your recommendations and then saying nothing, and just waiting to hear from the customer. If you don't ask, you don't learn. Even if the answer may not be what you were hoping for, ask the question and move on.

Welcoming objections

When you ask for feedback, the response you get is usually an objection; so you should accept that people almost always object even when they are convinced they want to buy. There are complex reasons for this, and techniques for resolving objections will be explored in the next chapter. But for now, you should try to welcome the objection. If you had not given an opportunity for the objection to surface, it would have still existed in the customer's mind, and you would never have closed the deal. With the objection out in the open, you have a chance to work with the customer to resolve it.

66 I would appreciate some feedback 99

Asking open questions

You will get better feedback if you ask the right questions. It's hard to rebound from a blunt "No" so use open-ended questions to elicit responses from the customer that you can work with. Your questions should be non-manipulative and quite straightforward: slippery sales patter like "Sounds pretty good doesn't it?" may antagonize the customer, so frame questions in a way that maintains the high level of dialogue used to this point.

Tip

GET YOUR TIMING RIGHT

You can ask for **feedback** at any time in your presentation. It's best to **wait** until you are **finished** so you don't get derailed, but if you suspect that the **customer** has a strong concern, **ask** for **feedback** earlier.

66 I've been talking for a while; now I'd love to hear from you 99

"What do you think about our recommendation?"

66 How does that sound? 99

Concluding
the sale

Resolving objections is often the most challenging part of the sales process – it can be uncomfortable and unpredictable. However, understanding the situation and practising your responses will help you perform well when you encounter resistance.

68 | UNDERSTANDING OBJECTIONS

72 | COLLECTING THE DATA

78 | REFRAMING OBJECTIONS

80 | DISCUSSING PRICE

84 | RESPONDING TO OBJECTIONS

86 | CLOSING THE SALE

92 | MOVING BEYOND THE CLOSE

04

Understanding objections

Up to this point in the needs-driven selling model, your role has been that of facilitator and advisor. Now, when you start to encounter objections from the client, the role can feel a lot more like selling. However, there's no reason to freeze and miss the opportunity.

Making decisions

Most people object to a selling proposal even though they are interested in buying. It's human nature. The lesson to learn is that not all objections are as bad as they first appear, and most can be resolved.

So why do buyers object when they're ready to buy? Most are simply looking for reassurance from the salesperson; they want to feel like they are making good, thoughtful, reasonable decisions, and they don't want to think that they are being hasty or foolish. They know that they will start questioning themselves soon after they make the purchase.

Recognizing hesitation

You may have heard some of the terms associated with this phenomenon of worry and hesitation, such as buyer's remorse and cognitive dissonance.

80%
of **successful sales** are only **agreed** after the **salesperson** has **five follow-up phone conversations with the customer** from the time of the **initial meeting**

This is a feeling of tension that arises when you keep two conflicting thoughts in mind simultaneously. When you make a decision to buy, especially when spending a lot of money, you may experience a sense of disequilibrium. Part of you feels good about the purchase, but part of you is not so sure. This is not a comfortable feeling. Professional buyers are also subject to similar feelings, so to protect themselves and feel as though they are doing the right thing, they object – even when they may be ready to buy.

> Why do buyers **object** when they're **ready to buy**? Most are simply **looking** for **reassurance**; they want to feel like they are making **good, thoughtful, reasonable decisions**

REACTING TO RESISTANCE

Most salespeople react in one of three ways when faced with objections – becoming defensive, aggressive, or simply giving up. None of these reactions is constructive, and none is likely to help you close the deal. To stop falling into one of these traps, and do what you do best – problem solve with the potential customer.

The three negative responses to resistance

BECOMING AGGRESSIVE

If you become confrontational and argumentative it suggests that you must **convince** the customer you're right – and by implication that they are wrong. This aggressive behaviour will not **encourage discussion and openess**.

01

GETTING DEFENSIVE

Going on the defensive and closing off further discussion with your potential new customer by justifying your position will not work. Adopting this negative stance **sends out the message** that the process is more about you than the client.

02

BECOMING PASSIVE

Some salespeople simply walk away at the first indication of an objection or hesitation. However, giving up is the worst reaction of all, as most customers need to be convinced that they are making the best decision. For all you know there may be **considerable interest**.

03

In focus

JUSTIFYING DECISIONS
People's desire to resolve the cognitive dissonance that accompanies buying decisions is illuminated by an observation from the advertising industry. A person is more likely to read an advertisement for a major purchase – such as an automobile – after they have bought the product rather than before the purchase. Reading the ad reinforces the correctness of the decision made in the buyer's mind.

33%
of businesses believe it takes too long to **close a deal**

> **Tip**
>
> ### STEER TOWARDS A SOLUTION
> Think of yourself as a **facilitator** when you **resolve** objections. It's your job to lead the way as you **navigate** towards **resolution**.

Approaching conflict

DEVELOPING A PROCESS

Dealing with customers' objections is less daunting when you stick to a process derived from proven conflict-management techniques. This helps you focus on the objective, maintain your professionalism, and curbs your tendency to react too quickly.

FULFILLING NEEDS

Before introducing the objection-resolution model, there are two assumptions that you need to accept. Firstly, many, if not most, objections are unfulfilled needs. Needs are motivational in nature and when you don't meet them to the customer's satisfaction, they usually appear later as objections. Put another way, if you don't discover all the needs, you risk being blindsided later by an objection.

ASSESSING INTEREST

The second assumption – which may seem counterintuitive – is that most objections indicate interest at some level. Indifference and apathy are the reactions you want to see least in response to your recommendations. When the client complains about something, at least they care about the outcome. Taking the customer's objection as a good sign will encourage you to work to resolve it. It's a healthy way to approach conflict. You don't have to accept these assumptions at face value, but work with them and decide later whether or not you agree.

Introducing the process

When you encounter resistance, start by acknowledging what the customer has said without responding to it with offence or defence. Next, make sure that you have heard and understood the entire issue. Review what is troubling your customer in a discussion. Sometimes, you will simply need to paraphrase the objection to clarify it; or you may have to reframe the objection and transform it into a need that you can address.

> Sometimes, you will **need** to paraphrase the objection to **clarify it**; or you may have to **reframe** the objection and **transform it** into a need that **you can address**

Addressing concerns

Next, address the concern as effectively as you can in order to resolve it. If the customer accepts your response, you should determine if there are other concerns. If there are, then repeat the process. If there are none, close the sale.

Resolving objections is a clear, linear process, you don't have to use every step to succeed, but having a well-defined process will help you deal with one of the hardest components of the sales process.

ASK YOURSELF...
About your buying behaviour   **YES   NO**

You can learn about your client's attitudes by reviewing how you react when you make a significant purchase:

1 Do I come up with **specific reasons** to delay or prevent a buying decision?... ☐ ☐

2 Is my **behaviour** shaped by the salesperson? .... ☐ ☐

3 Do I object because it helps me **feel more confident** about my purchase? .... ☐ ☐

4 Do I object because I want **to test** the salesperson?........ ☐ ☐

5 Do I **react well** to an aggressive sell?............................. ☐ ☐

Collecting the data

The first two steps in the objection resolution process involve you acknowledging the client's objections and asking them to elaborate on their concerns. Posing the right questions helps you collect the critical data you need to understand and deal with the customer's objection.

Acknowledging objections

Your aim at this point is to encourage your customer to open up about their objections. To begin this process, you should acknowledge their concerns: this doesn't mean agreeing with their objections (which would suggest a lack of conviction on your part) or implying that you disagree (which would set the scene for confrontation). Instead, simply recognize their right to object, demonstrate empathy, and show that you are amenable to discussing the situation. The customer will see that you are willing, and hopefully able, to solve the problem.

Understanding concerns

"I appreciate that investing in our system may seem daunting..."

"I appreciate your candour..."

"That's a fair question..."

"I think I understand why you might feel that way based on what you've heard so far..."

Using the right words

A good technique for acknowledging objections is to reflect the customer's own language in your response. Aim to paraphrase their objection, without being patronizing. For example, if the customer brings up the objection that your product is far too expensive for their budget, you could reply by saying "I recognize that expense is a major concern for you." Shown below are some examples of the types of phrases you can use to acknowledge objections.

Recognize their **right** to object, **demonstrate empathy**, and show that you are **amenable to discussing** the situation

"I can see why..."

77%

of **customers** buy products or services in order to **solve their problems**

Tip

TRANSFER YOUR SKILLS
Acknowledging is more than just a tool for use in the selling process – it is a **life skill**. Use it with your significant others, **colleagues**, **children**, even strangers. When you **acknowledge** how someone **may feel**, **good things** usually follow.

Questioning the client

The customer's stated objections are often just the tip of the iceberg. The issues they raise with you may not be expressing all their concerns, or may be masking their true objections. To get to the bottom of their concerns, you need to start asking more focused, deeper questions. Keep these questions crisp, open-ended, and void of content so that you do not suggest your own answers and so "lead the witness".

For example, if a client voices a general objection, do not immediately respond by asking, "Is it the price?" This specific question will succeed only in making the customer suspicious of the price quoted – you will have just given them another reason not to buy! Instead, try something such as: "Could you be more specific?" This type of question will encourage the customer to elaborate without giving them new reasons to object.

Questioning with care

"How come?"

"Can you say a little more about that?"

44%

of salespeople do not **contact** a lead after an initial rejection, **22%** give up after the second **14%** after the third

"I'm not sure I understand. Could you clarify?"

Tip

BE RESTRAINED
Do not go too far in **expressing** your desire to **work with** a prospect – it can work against you.

Being sensitive

When you deal with the client's objections, don't forget that you are in conflict resolution mode and sensitivity on your part is not only desirable but critical. The questioning process must not seem like an interrogation – it needs to be a comfortable experience for the customer so he or she will explain their concerns and continue the dialogue. Like so many of the factors that impact the sales process, it's how you do it that matters most.

"Would you please elaborate?"

Keep these **questions crisp, open-ended,** and void of **content**

ASKING QUESTIONS

Dos	Don'ts
O Being objective	O Appearing judgemental
O Staying in control	O Displaying emotion
O Asking open-ended questions	O Asking leading questions or patronizing the client
O Being straightforward	O Being perceived as manipulative
O Using appreciative phrases	O Being an interrogator

Accepting objections

Of course, there are times when you should agree with what the customer is saying, but without closing off the conversation. For example, if your product is more expensive than the competition's and you are unable to offer any discount on the stated price, your reply could be: "Yes, it is an expensive product, but I hope you think it's worth discussing its cost in respect of what it can do for you."

Encouraging the customer to open up

BE POSITIVE

Let your customer know that you **appreciate their insights** by interspersing your questions with appreciative phrases such as: "Thank you" and "That's very helpful".

BE DIRECT

Clearly signal your intentions using phrases such as: "I'd like to ask another question or two in order to..." to make the climate more **conducive** to problem solving.

In focus

CROSSING THE LINE

Almost any positive behaviour can become a negative one when used in excess. It's great to be curious until you become nosy. You should be assertive but not aggressive. By all means be pleasant; but stay away from obsequious. Be empathetic and customer focused, but do not appear to be patronizing.

Take a position, but resist becoming dogmatic. And of course be tenacious, just don't get stubborn. These distinctions become particularly important when resolving conflict, but if you trust your instincts and build on them with experience, you'll be right a lot more often than you'll be wrong.

MIRROR THE CLIENT

If the client becomes obstructive and puts you on the back foot, try **mirroring** his or her objections. For example, counter "Your suggestion is ridiculous" with "Why do you think this seems ridiculous?" Do this in **a non-judgemental way** that conveys your **real curiosity** about the answer.

INTRODUCE YOUR QUESTIONS

Give reasons for why you need the **information** to help to diffuse suspicion and put the **customer at ease.** If your customer raises the objection that your solution is complicated, respond with: "Yes, it is complex – but it's also very manageable. Can we discuss this further…?"

BE SILENT

Sometimes, and especially when a client reacts in an inappropriately strong manner, being silent is the **best option.** Silence can **defuse the situation** and give the client time to realize that his or her behaviour is not contributing to **a resolution**.

Reframing objections

By this time, you have heard the customer's objections to your proposal. Most – but not all – objections that you will hear from clients are really disguised, unfulfilled needs. So the next step of the selling process is reframing the objections as needs.

Translating into needs

Objections from customers are barriers to progress, whereas needs are aspirational, so it follows that turning objections into needs makes them easier to discuss and resolve. These examples illustrate how objections in fact mask needs:

- A client complains about the high complexity of your proposal: what he may need is a clearer explanation of how it works pitched at his own level.
- A client recounts a bad experience of a purchase similar to the one you are proposing: what she may need is reassurance that it will not happen again.
- A client laments the difficulty of changing their in-house systems: he may need to understand that you can help to facilitate the process.

"I bought something similar and it didn't work"

"Don't worry, this is a completely new, improved model"

"We'll need to change our in-house systems"

"Let me help you with that"

"Your proposal is too complicated"

"Let me explain how it will work"

Case study

REFRAMING FOR SUCCESS

Reframing is not restricted to selling situations. A multi-billion dollar company was in the process of selecting a new CEO: during the interviews, one of the leading candidates was challenged by the chairman. The candidate had a reputation for risk taking, and the chairman expressed his worries about his judgement in financial decisions. The candidate's reframe went something like this: "My impression is that you're concerned about my reputation for trying new things and need to feel comfortable that when it comes to financial decisions I will demonstrate the fiduciary responsibility that the job demands. Is that correct?" He gave a great response and two days later he got the job.

Sounding positive

Reframing is the art of turning a negative concept into a positive, and so changing the apparently unresolvable into the possible. You can reframe almost any objection into an invitational question that asks how something can be done as opposed to why it can't. An objection like "My manager will never go for this" becomes "It appears to me that there's a need to establish a rock-solid business case for this purchase."

When you reframe a client's objection you are changing the tone of what they said, and you should avoid putting words into their mouth – note the use of the phrase "it appears to me" opening the example response above.

> You can **reframe** almost any objection into **an invitational question** that **asks how** something **can be done** as opposed to why it can't

Tip

KEEP TRYING
Don't worry if the way you **reframe the objection** is off target. **Ask the customer** to correct you and keep trying until you **get it right**.

Setting objectives

When you reframe the concern as a need, make sure it is a need that you are able to address. For example, don't say something like "It seems like you need to get a lower price" if you can't move on price. Instead, try "As I understand, you need to see more clearly the cost/value equation here."

After you have reframed the objection, confirm with the customer that they agree with your interpretation. You have now converted their objection into a new objective – with the client's agreement you can now move towards meeting the objective and edge closer to closing the deal.

Discussing price

Customers will always complain about price. Indeed, price resistance is the most common objection salespeople will encounter, and can be the hardest to resolve. However, as with other types of objection, understanding why the customer is objecting and turning that objection into a need can be an effective way of managing the resistance.

Understanding price resistance

Everyone wants to find a good deal and feel like they are getting a keen price. However, objections about price are sometimes used as a convenient and acceptable reason to object; they are a smokescreen to mask other issues. In these situations, it is important that you question your customer to determine what the underlying issue really is. At other times, the objection truly is all about price. In instances where the buyer is making his or her decision on price alone, there may be little leeway for negotiation, and you may choose to walk away from the relationship.

Everyone wants to find a **good deal** and feel like they are getting **a keen price**

88% of consumers buy a brand for **quality**; 50% buy for **price**

Pre-empting the objection

If you have undergone a thorough needs determination process, your customer should not be surprised or shocked about the price you propose. Needs determination should include a discussion about how much the customer is currently paying or expects to pay. Questioning the customer about their budget or pricing guidelines will help you recommend a price that is close to what is expected. If the customer won't answer your questions, give them a "sense of" cost: "Just so you know, a programme like this typically costs £100. How does that sound?" You will quickly find out whether this is a long way from what they expect to pay.

Tip

BE CLEAR ABOUT THE VALUE
Don't confuse **price with value:** people are willing to pay more if they **understand** the **value** they are getting for their money.

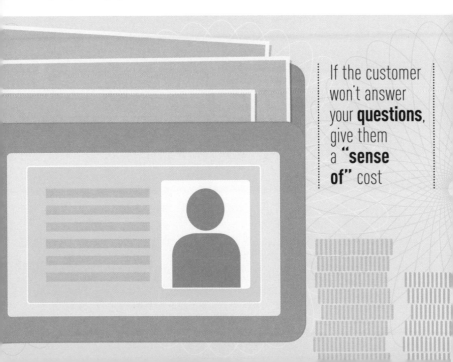

If the customer won't answer your **questions**, give them a **"sense of"** cost

Resolving price objections

The objection-resolution process is your best tool in dealing with price objections. Firstly, acknowledge the objection as you would any other, for example: "I know you are trying to keep costs down." Next, get the customer talking. Ask questions, and find out about any other offers they have had from your competitors – how do they compare to yours? Are the deals comparable with yours in terms of the value delivered? Learn as much as you can regarding how far off you are in price from other offers.

> If the customer **agrees** with your reframe, **address the need**. An objection often turns out to be less significant than it **appeared** to be

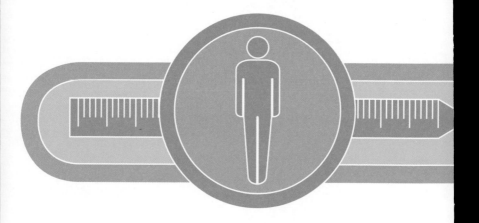

CHOOSE YOUR QUESTIONS CAREFULLY
Getting a customer to **elaborate** about price or cost issues is a **delicate matter.** Be sensitive in your approach, using questions such as "How far off are we?" or "Can you tell us a bit more?"

50%

of **consumers** visit **discount retailers** for the **best priced goods**; **47%** of shoppers visit to **see what is new**

Reframing the issue

When resolving price objections, reframing the objection is critical. Do everything you can to turn your customer's objection into need, using phrases such as: "So if I understand you correctly, you need to know exactly what you will get for the additional 10 per cent", "My understanding is that you need to understand why we charge a bit more than X and why it's still in your interest to buy from us...", or "It appears to me that you need to feel comfortable with your decision to pay us more than some of our competitors..."

If the customer agrees with your reframe, go ahead and address the need. Give it your best shot, and see if they will accept your point of view. You will be surprised how an objection often turns out to be less significant than it originally appeared to be.

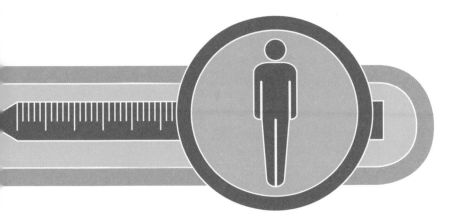

In focus

LOWERING YOUR PRICE

The last thing you should do is lower your price without taking something off the table. If you provide a quote and a customer objects and you then subsequently drop your price, the message is clear – you were charging too much originally. This sentiment can have serious negative impact on further business and how you are perceived. If you do have to lower your price (which happens), let the customer know what you have to remove or reduce from the original proposal. As a last resort, let them know you are lowering the price to earn your way in, but that the original price was fair and this is a short-term offer that you will not repeat.

Responding to objections

Once you have reformulated your customer's objection into a need, it's time to respond. Usually, this is straightforward – the answers lie in what you have already proposed and in knowledge you already have – but sometimes you will need to be creative in order to lead your client to a solution.

Playing to your strengths

Before you can move to the final stage of the selling process – closing the sale – you need to deal definitively with all of the customer's objections (or their unfulfilled needs, as we know them). You may need to use all the means at your disposal to achieve this essential goal (see the process opposite). If you still cannot resolve the customer's hesitations, concerns, and objections, you will need to revert to problem-solving mode to find a creative solution. If you still draw a blank, call time out and ask for a break to explore possibilities. Make an appointment to come back in a day or two with fresh ideas to move forward. Your customer will respect you for taking the time to consider his or her issues in the long run.

Tip

BE RELAXED
Remember that some questions customers ask are not objections – simply **plain questions.** Just because someone asks you about inventory issues doesn't necessarily mean they are worried about them.

Questioning effectively

Your final act in the objection-resolution process is to learn if there are other objections. This may sound like opening Pandora's Box, but it's critical. If other objections do exist, you need to learn about them because if you fail to uncover them now, they will certainly spoil the deal later. So ask the question. Keep your enquiry neutral and use expressions like: "Is there anything else we need to discuss?" Try to stay away from negative language and terms such as "objections", or "issues", or "concerns". If you use words like these, you can give the customer the impression that you know something that they don't. Keep it simple. If objections remain, repeat the process until you have removed all the obstacles that stand in the way of closing.

Your final **act** in the objection-resolution process is to **learn** if there are other objections. You **need to learn** about them because if you fail to **uncover** them now, they will certainly spoil **the deal** later

Closing in on closing

HIGHLIGHT THE SPECIFIC BENEFITS

Repeat or **rephrase a benefit** the client has forgotten or did not fully **appreciate** during the earlier presentation phase.

REVIEW THE FEATURES AND BENEFITS

Go back over these **trusted** selling tools.

SELL YOURSELF

Make your **customer** feel confident in your **ability**. Explain why you're so **well placed** to **address** their concerns about service, quality, or specification.

PRAISE YOUR COLLEAGUES

Make sure that the customer knows that you're part of a **dedicted** and **responsive** team.

GET CREATIVE

Generate ideas together with your client to modify the strategy: use inclusive language when **describing** how to **overcome** objections: "we have to figure out why..." or "our priority is now to..."

PRAISE YOUR COMPANY

Talk about your company's history, **successes**, and commitment to **excellence**.

CREATE CONFIDENCE IN YOUR SOLUTIONS

Review similar problems that you have **solved** for other clients.

Closing the sale

Over the years, salespeople's ingenuity has given life to scores of "sure-fire" closing techniques. Going by names such as the Puppy-dog Close, the Distraction Close, and the Treat Close, some are just gimmicky, while others border on the manipulative. Their faults lie in the fact that they all see closing as a special technique, rather than the natural outcome of a problem-solving dialogue with the client.

Approaching the close

You have built the relationship, determined the needs, made great recommendations, and resolved the customer's objections. It's time to close – to ask for the business. So why do so many sales professionals find this step so difficult? The answer is simple – it is the fear of rejection appearing once again. This fear pushes many experienced salespeople towards canned "closes", like the Specific Terms Close, where the idea is to present the customer with a prearranged buying scenario, and then ask them to agree to it. For example, "We can deliver 10 palettes on 12 May for $1,000 – is that OK?" Of course, on occasion, this approach – and others in a similar vein – may bring about a sale, but often the customer will think you presumptive and rude. It's canned selling at its lowest.

16%

of customers are likely to **believe product claims** that are backed by a **scientist or other expert**

Tip

BE GRACIOUS
Always thank the customer for their **business** – it is vital to show that you are grateful.

SALESPERSON
"Anything else we need to discuss?"

Assuming the best

To close a deal you shouldn't need to rely on corny closing tactics. You need simply to demonstrate the same credibility, integrity, and degree of interaction with the customer that you showed throughout the selling process. Don't change the basis of your hard-won relationship at this point.

Assume that if the customer does not have a reason not to buy, he or she is ready to buy. This is called the Assumptive Close. In the Assumptive Close, illustrated below, the dialogue with the customer is direct.

The point is clear even though the words you choose may vary: you ask the customer if there are other concerns. If they say no, then you double check. If everything seems OK, just ask for the customer for the business.

Assume that if the customer does not **have a reason** not to buy, he or she is **ready to buy**. This is **called** the Assumptive Close

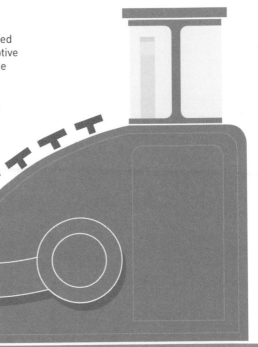

CUSTOMER
"No, not that I can think of."

SALESPERSON
"So everything seems OK?"

CUSTOMER
"Yes, I believe so."

SALESPERSON
"Great, then how do we get started?"

Asking and getting

If you've done your job well up to this point, the customer will know that you have something valuable to offer and will want to buy from you; moreover they will want you to ask for their business. If you don't, you're expecting the customer to do your job. It seems obvious, but if you don't ask for the business, you're much less likely to get it.

Once there has been a commitment to buy, close the sale by beginning to pin down the specifics. A good way to cover all the key variables is to answer the "four Ws" – who will do what by when with help from whom? When you have the answers to these questions, you are ready to execute.

Close the sale by beginning to pin down the **specifics**. A good way to cover all the **key variables** is to answer the **"four Ws"**

Consolidating the close

Everyone needs reassurance after making a large purchase – to silence the nagging voice asking if they did the right thing (discussed earlier in this chapter). With this in mind, it is important to make sure you are highly visible to the customer after you have closed the deal.

33

days is the time **Brazilians** need to close a deal; **Dutch** salespeople take **52 days**

Deal or no deal

If you don't close the deal – and of course you won't always – it is vital to keep the momentum of the selling process going. Set objectives for resolving issues and be clear about what has to be done before the next meeting. Experienced salespeople will tell you that the only time you fail in a sales call is when you don't get a next step, so make it your priority to keep channels of communication open.

Set objectives for resolving issues and **be clear** about what has to be done

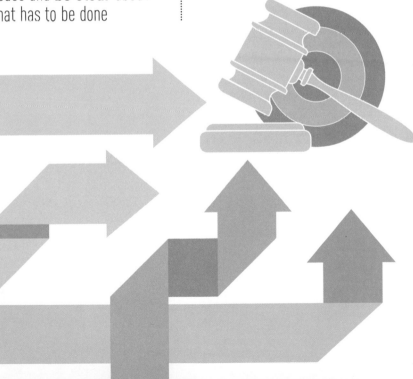

Caring for clients

Some salespeople say that "the real selling starts after you get the business", and it is very hard to argue with that sentiment. With hard work, anyone can get the first order; it's the ones who get the second, third, and fourth who are most successful. Whatever you do, do not fall into the stereotypical image of a "love 'em and leave 'em" salesperson. If you do, your relationship will be a short one. Guaranteed!

30%

increase in customer interaction may result when they are **rewarded** with **loyalty** programmes

Respecting power

To be successful repeatedly, you need to acknowledge the transfer of power that occurs when the deal is closed. When a customer is a prospect, they hold all the cards, but once they commit to the deal, they lose some of that power as they are dependent upon you to deliver. It's uncomfortable for them, and it is a good reason for you to show humility after closing the deal – it's not the time to whoop and punch the air.

Collecting for success

There is a distasteful acronym out there in the world of selling – ABC, Always Be Closing – that reflects the strong emphasis placed on closing by many sales managers. Of course, closing is important, but it shouldn't be viewed as an isolated aim. Transform this unhealthy acronym into an ABC that will help you – Always Be Collecting: only when you consistently question, understand, and resolve issues together with your customer will you be on the road to success.

Anyone can get the **first order**; it's the ones who get the second, third, and fourth who are **most successful**

CASE STUDY

USING A "CLOSER"

A young salesman had called on the same client twice a month for two years. Sensing he was close to his first order, he brought his boss with him. The junior salesman reviewed price agreements, credit terms, and product specifications with the client. He kept asking the customer if everything was approved, whether they were satisfied, and if there were any other questions. All the answers were positive, but the salesman just couldn't pull the trigger. Finally, the manager lost patience and blurted out "Well then, how about an order?" The customer's response was "What took you so long to ask?"

The customer was obviously ready to buy and the young salesman's reluctance to close was only raising suspicions in the client's mind. If the manager had not stepped in, the sale could have been lost.

However, using a more senior person as a "closer" is a poor selling model. The salesperson should always feel adequately equipped, trained, and empowered by his organization to confidently ask for the business.

Moving beyond the close

After you have closed, you earn yet another great opportunity to differentiate yourself from the competition. Following through goes beyond just following up on your promises – doing what you said you would do professionally and on time. Following through means exceeding what's expected of you and so sending the clear message to your customers that you are consistently thinking about them.

Following up

Follow-up is doing whatever you had committed to do at the end of the sales meeting with your customer. It is a process that you initiate to ensure that objectives are accomplished and commitments are fulfilled.

It is your responsibility to make sure that all of your organization's resources are doing what is needed to move the relationship to the next level. Will the samples be there on time? Is everyone aware of and able to meet the agreed delivery dates? Is the team committed to participate in the next meeting?

Confirming next steps

Every single sales call you make – from a brief catch-up meeting to a formal presentation – deserves a follow-up email. This can be sent in the form of a regular email, a formal letter, or even a hand-written note – whatever suits both your style and the occasion – but it must follow every call. The follow-up message should thank the customer for their time, review what was discussed, and define the next steps. It can also serve as a reminder of who has committed to do what and by when.

Follow-up is a process that **you initiate** to **ensure** that **objectives** are **accomplished** and **commitments** are **fulfilled**

MAKING THE MARK

Dos	Don'ts
O Promising and delivering	O Overpromising and underdelivering
O Putting it in writing	O Assuming the customer understands
O Being visible	O Being a nuisance
O Being consistently professional	O Forgetting details
O Showing interest in doing business	O Appearing desperate or over anxious

Keeping in contact

When you follow through, you do more than you need to. Here are some ways you can surprise your customers with your level of commitment:

- Regularly check how things are progressing internally, and communicate effectively to all involved on a day-to-day basis.
- Send your customers a list of follow-up activities and deliverables, including dates; make sure you meet them consistently.
- Let your customer know well in advance if for some reason you can't meet a deliverable.
- Send emails updating your customers without requesting a response. This instils confidence that you have their interests in mind all the time.

70%

of consumers said they would **spend more** with companies that gave excellent **service**

In focus

TRACKING CONTACT

Time speeds by. It's not hard for 90 days to pass before you realize that you haven't made any contact with a customer. "Out of sight... out of mind" may be a cliché, but it's true: and if you haven't been in touch with a client, it's a safe bet that your competitor has. To prevent long silences, track how often you make contact with your customers. Use a spreadsheet, online tracker, or whatever suits your style to record every face-to-face meeting, as well as all the phone calls, letters, and emails.

Index

A

acknowledging objections 73
Active Listening 49
agenda, sales meeting 41
aggression, dealing with
objections 69
appointments, making 36
assertiveness 77
Assumptive Close 87

B

benefits
focus on 58–59, 60
highlighting, in response to
objections 85
joint sales meetings 55
unique 60
big-picture questions 42, 44
brainstorming 51
brochures 60
business needs 31
buyers *see* customers

C

Citibank 33
"closers" 91
closing techniques 85, 86–91
Coca Cola 45
cognitive dissonance 68, 69
cold calls 36
colleagues
expert help 71
feedback from 35, 55
joint sales meetings 54–55
praising, in response to
objections 85
commitment, winning 14
complacency 33
confidence 14
conflict resolution 70, 74–77
consolidating close 89
Consumer Banking Group 33
creativity
problem-solving 10, 50–51
responding to objections 85
credentials presentation 38–39
curiosity 11, 77
customers
added value expectations
10–13, 63
appealing to 16–21
becoming complacent
about 33
buyer's remorse 68

customers (cont.)
buying behaviour 71
buying decisions 16–17, 68
closing the sale 85, 86–91
commitment, winning 14
credentials presentation
38–39
feedback from 64–65
follow-up 92
following through 93
ideas, offering new 62–63
joint sales meetings 54–55
keeping in contact 93
listening skills 48–49
needs-based selling *see*
needs-based selling
objections, dealing with
see objections
planning approach 34–35
price discussions 80–83
problem-solving *see*
problem-solving
recommendations, making
58–65
risk averse 30
sales meetings *see* sales
meetings
surprising 23
targeting the pitch 60–61

D

decisions, buying 16–17, 68
defensiveness, dealing with
objections 69
differentiating yourself 22–23

E

80/20 rule, breaking 26
emails 36, 37, 92, 93
empathy, showing 17,
31, 72
exit strategy, and risk
management 20

F

fact-finding questions
42, 47
features
in client presentations
58–59
highlighting–in response to
objections 85
targeting the pitch
60–61

feedback
from colleagues 35, 55
from customers 64–65
follow-up 92
following through 93

H

humility, showing 27

I

ideas, offering new 62–63
information
planning approach
34, 35
prioritizing messages 60
questioning customers *see*
questions
understanding objections
77
initial contacts 36–37
interest assessment, and
objections 70
interviewers, television,
learning from 43

J

joint sales meetings 54–55
justifying decisions 69

L

lateral thinking 51
leads 36
letters, customer contact 22,
36, 92
Levitt, Theodore 28
listening skills 48–49

M

Maister, David 17
meetings *see* sales meetings
mirroring objections 77

N

needs-based selling 14–15
business and personal
needs 31
credentials, presenting
38–39
joint sales meetings 54–55
listening skills 48–49
making first move 36–37
objections, dealing with *see*
objections
planning approach 34–35

needs (cont.)
    problem-solving *see*
        problem-solving
    questioning for 27, 42–47
    recognizing needs 28–33
    reviewing 52–53
    sales meeting 40–41
    understanding needs 26–55
    unfulfilled needs 70

O

objections
    accepting 76
    conflict resolution 70,
        74–77
    data collection 72–73
    dealing with 68–71
    interest assessment 70
    mirroring 77
    pre-empting 81
    price-related 80–83
    reframing 78–79, 83
    resolving and closing sale
        70–71, 74–75
    responding to 84–85
    understanding 68–71
open questions, feedback 65
Osborn, Alex 51

P

passivity, dealing with
    objections 69
Pepsi Cola 45
personal needs 31
personality, salespeople 12–13
Peters, Tom 23
pitch, targeting 60–61
planning approach 34–35
presentations 58–59
    confident 14
    credentials 38–39
    rehearsal 35
price
    lowering 83
    objections 80–83
    and value, difference
        between 81
prioritizing information 60
problem-solving 10, 50–51
    brainstorming 51
    compared with selling 14
    resolving objections 70–71,
        74–75

Q

questions
    big-picture 42, 44
    fact-finding 42, 47
    needs-based selling 27,
        42–47
    open, and feedback 65

R

rapport, building 40
recommendations, making
    58–65
reframing objections 78–79, 83
relationship building 10–23
research, importance of 34–35
resistance *see* objections
respect, gaining 18
reviewing needs 52–53
risk
    management 20–21
    risk averse customers 30
    willingness to take 12
Rogers, Carl 52
role
    in sales meeting 41, 54
    as salesperson 11

S

sales meetings
    closing techniques 85,
        86–91
    feedback *see* feedback
    follow-up 92
    holding 40–41
    ideas, offering new
        62–63
    initial contacts 36–37
    joint 54–55
    listening skills 48–49
    needs-based selling *see*
        needs-based selling
    objections, dealing with *see*
        objections
    problem-solving *see*
        problem-solving
    questions *see* questions
    role in 41, 54
    targeting the pitch
        60–61
    see also customers
salespeople
    credentials presentation
        38–39

salespeople (cont.)
    differentiating yourself
        22–23
    ideas, offering new 62–63
    objections, dealing with *see*
        objections
    personality 12–13
    recommendations, making
        58–65
    role of 11
    selling yourself 84
silence, in response to
    objections 77
social media 10, 36
surprising your customers 23

T

targeting the pitch 60–61
television interviewers,
    learning from 43
thought process, analyzing 28
trust building 18–21

U

uncompensated ideas 62–63

V

value
    adding 10–13, 63
    and price, difference
        between 81
visibility, achieving 22, 89

W

"WOW!" factor 23

Acknowledgments

Dedication
I dedicate this to my family who by far are the most important people in my life. Everything good that has happened to me begins with Lois, my wife for almost 40 years. She is my best friend, my consistent source of inspiration, my biggest cheerleader, and my stabilizing influence. She is also the nicest person I know.

My daughters, Andrea Cooper and Deborah Rubin, are living proof that your children do in fact grow up and become your best friends. Everything I do in life is magnified by the joy they provide every day. Their husbands, Jon and Howie, are marvellous citizens of the world and their spectacular children, Logan, Sage, and Jonah, generate feelings that I could not possibly put in words.

Author's acknowledgments
I begin by thanking Cobalt id, who enabled me to put in writing much of what we have learned from our research during the last 30 years. Marek Walisiewicz has been an outstanding resource, and I am most grateful to him for his support. I am gratified and thrilled that Dorling Kindersley chose to publish this book as I have always admired this extraordinary organization. Stephanie Katz is an outstanding editor who can transform the dullest verbiage into an interesting story. I admire her skills, appreciate her friendship, and thank her for her contributions. Francine Mendence and Doris Anderson run The Baron Group and have stretched even beyond their extraordinary limits to help make this happen.

And finally, whenever I look at what I have been able to accomplish, all roads lead to Synectics® Inc. and the five wonderful years I spent at that marvellous organization. Rick Harriman, my dear friend and colleague, made that possible, and I will never stop expressing my gratitude to him.

Publisher's acknowledgments
The publisher would like to thank Hilary Bird and Margaret McCormack for indexing, Judy Barratt for proofreading, Phil Gamble for design assistance, and Charles Wills for co-ordinating Americanization.

Original edition:
Senior Editor Peter Jones
Senior Art Editor Helen Spencer
Executive Managing Editor Adèle Hayward
Managing Art Editor Kat Mead
Art Director Peter Luff
Publisher Stephanie Jackson
Production Editor Ben Marcus
Production Controller Hema Gohil
US Editor Margaret Parrish

First edition produced for Dorling Kindersley Limited by Cobalt id
www.cobaltid.co.uk

Editors
Louise Abbott, Kati Dye, Maddy King, Marek Walisiewicz